LIBERAL
WITCHES

KAREN KELLOCK PH.D.

Manual for
Superior Men

**A complete theory based on Einstein physics,
Political Psychology, Systems Theory
and Archetypal Psychiatry.**

FORMULA
All success attraction
All disease obstruction
All recovery elimination

You must fast on all three
OBSTRUCTIONS:
People
Habit
Food

LIBERAL WITCHES

Jezebel Warning: The MINUTE she gets an edge she'll take over despite your distress.   When I went from an echo-chamber of adoring sycophants to a dungeon of liberal feminists I saw the radical difference.   Satan is jealous, it's the devil in all of us. But life is hell when faced with it especially in feminists. Instantly the women sized me up and squeezed me out. "Have nothing to do with her" they mocked. They target a scapegoat and won't let her up her entire life. Even after death grudges remain/eternal strife.   You hear of older sister wives beating the younger ones up. It's women so how could we doubt it.

LIBERAL WITCHES

THEY WON'T BE CORRECTED
THE TRIGGERING TRUTH
MALE-LOVING FEMALES ARE ENEMY
SELF-RIGHTEOUS INDIGNATION
MEN ARE HUNTERS
DON'T LET EM IN
THEY BRING AN ARMY
DROP THE BORROWERS
SECOND NATURE LEANERS
THEY'RE LIKE THE GESTAPO
THE TABLES HAVE TURNED
MODERN FEMALE NARCISSISTS
SIMPLICITY IS GONE
GIRLS PUT DOWN MEN
HATE TRUMP/ALL ALPHA MALES
TRIGGERED FEMALES
THE DEGENERATION OF BLOODLINES
SHE'S BACK FROM STANFORD
INSANE MESSAGES OF FEMINISTS
DIONYSIAN MAD MAX
GOLDEN GIRLS: OLD SLUTS
HER GIRLFRIENDS COME FIRST
RAMPANT FEMALE SEX SIN

KAREN KELLOCK

LIBERAL WITCHES

LIBERAL WITCHES

These are liberal witches and they don't even know it. They are pagans and a bad influence: twits.

THEY WON'T BE CORRECTED

If the ego won't allow for correction and they're misled by feminist direction what is the outcome?

They don't understand that time changes all, that pretty privilege is only temporary then a fall.

It's all a result of the lack of male authority today. Docile or absent fathers, distracted moms gone away.

They're born with crazy mothers who divorced their fathers so how could they be anything other?

Everything that happens is the man's fault, tho' he had to leave because mom belongs in a crazy vault.

Was she driven to insanity? YES, by an interplay of extreme devaluation and privilege of the pretty.

The problem is all from a lack of male authority but to even say this makes them furious see.

THE TRIGGERING TRUTH

It's the triggering truth of this century: women are self-destructive without male authority.

They flaunt their brazen sexuality like it's a feather in their cap and proof of their superiority.

The smartest women listen to men. The dumbest show open disdain, it's all they're taught friend.

LIBERAL WITCHES

Men need women not to survive but for a solid family structure yet nothing's falling apart quicker.

Listen lady lunatics: men run the show/do the heavy lifting. They don't mind at all so stop bitching.

They like not listening to men with a bad girl image. Mean girl sarcasm make it all a challenge.

No father to put em in their place with boundaries, a mom who lets em run amuck, loud/crazy.

MALE-LOVING FEMALES ARE ENEMY

Any woman for male authority is seen as the ENEMY and she'd better watch for revenge see.

They won't listen to men just each other. Crazy stories trigger hatred of even their father or brother.

You don't have to die to stop these memories, just see it as a SYSTEM where you had no choice see.

Alcoholics--drunks--doing stupid degenerate stuff all the time and thinking it's funny, fun and fine.

Compare this to the fifties: we've come so far down the rabbit hole ladies and you were part of it see.

The guts needed to stand up for chastity is way beyond their capacity, it's easier to give in as "sexy".

SELF-RIGHTEOUS INDIGNATION

Demanding respect/appreciation in that shrill voice with self-righteous indignation all over her face.

It's this same teenager that screws up little boys as a mother later. Addictive homes = disorder.

LIBERAL WITCHES

When you help them they latch on like a parasite and won't let you go, calling you day and night.

He drains you and puts nothing back. You want a man who makes you a nice offer not a sad sack.

We create our own reality by what we ACCEPT into our energy producing a good and bad day.

Men are hunters: they know women LOVE to hear the words "I love you": it's like a magic key Sue.

MEN ARE HUNTERS

Men are hunters: they know women LOVE to hear the words "I love you": it's like a magic key Sue.

To get involved with men who've already been trained to overcome women with key words is insane.

A good man with resources won't be checkin' you out, lickin' his lips and spoutin' sexual talk.

A man with nothing to lose will approach in a flighty way but a good man with resources won't ok.

The 2 approaches are totally different. One worms his way in but a good man enters hat in hand.

One gives you an OFFER and you accept it or not. The other wants to ENTER to be taken care of.

The bad man hollers from his car to enter, the good man walks to your door and calls your dad "sir".

DON'T LET EM IN

You're happy as a lark one day, then you let him in tho' unannounced and all hell breaks loose ok.

LIBERAL WITCHES

If you're walking and he's in his car hollerin' you know that's not the one darlin', a good man be respectin'.

If you ask him not to bring his friends again and he does anyway: drop him and never let him in ok.

You don't need an army marching into your home. Speaking as a recluse I hated that the most.

In my youth I was never told these things and I was actually flattered being used by earthlings.

Ladies get into their forties & start settling while inside they know what's happening/are hurting.

THEY BRING AN ARMY

The mega-user gets in your house and then, what a surprise, at the door are all his friends.

Since TV's "Friends" the youth move in groups and they think nothing of bringing in the troops.

You got good herb? The whole town's at your door. You gotta hide/tell em your family's coming over.

The best description is "they wanna piece of me". You feel em grabbing at you spiritually too see.

The grabby "sucking spirit" dies the minute you're married. You're free, no one does that now see.

The sucking spirit wants to borrow or destroy all that you have. You can feel they want it bad.

DROP THE BORROWERS

The worst are the immature female borrowers. Cut these off and elevate up to your investors.

LIBERAL WITCHES

If you're good looking they hate your darling but will hang on for reflected glory while using.

If you have high goals don't settle for losers but find a similar cruiser and be a coat tail rider.

If you say you don't let men in your house when alone and he argues shut the door, it's proven.

They want money: go to a bank. They want to do laundry: go to a laundromat. You had to do that!

SECOND NATURE LEANERS

It's second nature to lean on mom, which is you. They think nothing of it if you don't either Sue.

If you say you don't let men in your house when alone and he argues shut the door [you've grown].

The older we get the more they lean. Surely grandma will let em take advantage they think.

No one helped you when you were down and you've grown. Now don't let em in/go back down.

Women often use men. They have the key to their computer but it's a severe regression for them.

To have em in my house was a shock. I create an otherworldly environment which was blocked.

There are so many women--loser ladies--who will fall for this, that's why men continue to do it sis.

It was before a fence I experienced this. You gotta have a wall so they can't GET to your door sis.

THEY'RE LIKE THE GESTAPO

LIBERAL WITCHES

It's like the gestapo coming to the door. Losing privacy and independence is terrible in war.

Dad schooled me on the Scottish highlanders, so independent they fenced with molts and rivers.

People expect you to do their thing and if in control they'll demand it of you pathetic underlings.

I don't like things imposed on me and that's all I felt when I had to live with thee: pure misery.

The lower is always imposing on the higher. We have sensibilities and they are ok in the gutter.

I can't go to a monastery without feeling some kind of tyranny, it has to be real independence see.

THE TABLES HAVE TURNED

It's the style for women not to need men now. They're deliberately mean so if you're nice, wow!

We all gotta mate, we just don't know where he is. Beating the bushes won't find him so quit it sis.

Once he's won your heart, paying and in the house you can treat him liket he king he is for now.

Stop trying to approach men. Just be a better woman then ask God for what you desire, amen.

Then, if the man hasn't appeared yet you simply continue on your upward path for it.

If a man is too much for you simply raise your frequency. Its on YOU where you put your vital energy.

The greatest don't have 200 friends but a small circle where they're always happy--make sense?

LIBERAL WITCHES

A dignified lady can be as introverted as she wants since the man is the hunter for response.

You don't have to exert energy, just raise your frequency. It's as simple as that for birds and bees.

The narcissist expects women to attract to him. To hell with this! Man is the initiator or forget him sis.

Know who are and be confident. Men will flood to you cuz you are a happy woman and different.

Women today have an overwhelming amount of mental issues cuz most have been molested too.

MODERN FEMALE NARCISSISTS

These modern females show narcissism on a whole new spectrum and you will get very burnt man.

Women have issues and put their past stuff on you. It aint gonna happen you should say to Sue.

Women are damaged as teenagers. Just listen to the boys talk but the girls are much worse sir.

Nothing feels pure anymore. The girls talk to one but were already talking to someone else sooner.

If she's into a boy she'll deliberately be aloof. Game playing is big with teens and it gets cruel.

The toxic stuff wastes your brain cells, energy and very life. Yet it's all toxic and I recall it well, aye.

SIMPLICITY IS GONE

It's WILD and completely different from the simple life of the past. Add in dating sites, it's a mess.

LIBERAL WITCHES

She's with one but is concerned what a prior boyfriend thinks of her. For young men things get weird.

They're psychotically narcissistic and egotistical. It's a spectacle but one you don't want to know.

But in society's eyes MEN are the bad people tho' they're doing what's right in the face of evil.

I lay the blame on sex sin. Sin brings symptoms and the girls show consequences of dalliances.

GIRLS PUT DOWN MEN

The girls say men are of no value--they're just pigs or mules--and each generation gets worse too.

As she starts to ruin his life, he EXITS then gets all the blame. This is a terrible situation ok.

When they see how messed up the girls are they can't stick around for the absurdities are profound.

No dad in the home, a feminist mother who's often gone and no moral teaching around sex at all.

The outcome is the anti-female spirit and insanity in women. Fits, rages and promiscuous abandon.

Paranoid psychosis in women: The police are going to kill them and men are dangerous vermin.

Defund the cops and ruin the men in divorce courts. Women now rule as everything turns to rot.

HATE TRUMP/ALL ALPHA MALES

Hate Trump and hate all alpha males. After three generations of this it's ingrained in girls.

LIBERAL WITCHES

After years of feminism they need psychotherapy. A complete rehab of their mental ways of seeing.

If they leave the sick relationship because they are the healthy ones, men are blamed from then on.

Serial fornication—one sick relationship after another—worsens the situation/is worse for women.

This myth that men are bad makes em more conciliatory after that and more abused as a consequence.

TRIGGERED FEMALES

Feminism destroyed the female character decades back and now it's entrenched to act like that.

Tell her she should do housework and she gets triggered. Any such remark lights war in her.

Being damaged they get good at hiding it. They know how to act somewhat when it calls for it.

What a world when you must be so careful about the women and research them first, amen?

When they're inevitably treated with disrespect it triggers them more and what a scare.

They shoot for commitment too fast and that's a red flag. They attach discouragement to you Jack.

THE DEGENERATION OF BLOODLINES

This is dyseugenics: the degeneration of bloodlines as falsehoods become ingrained and assigned.

Most men want relationship. "But it was him": no it was YOU feeling justified acting like a bitch.

LIBERAL WITCHES

After reversing outa feminism I couldn't even talk to women as logic brought the opposite reaction.

They appear online and a hundred men write them. What does that do to a narcissistic woman?

They rage fit easily and take it for granted it's the way to be as it's instantly confirmed by the ladies.

They give men trouble but their war on women is despicable. Having been targeted I recall it well.

Here comes the lies and slanders. That's how I felt talking to female haters, my name was slurred.

SHE'S BACK FROM STANFORD

Sister got back from Stanford--most liberal school--and targeted me until I went mad it was so cruel.

We were a Christian home and suddenly we were the enemy: that's the result of liberalism see.

They are so self-righteous because to them their cosmology is a tautology: a self-evident fact see.

What should we do, teach em to be sweet? That triggers them more having been taught these things.

I'm sorry for the boys but especially sorry for the girls. To be a psychotic witch is very uncomfortable.

They resent being told what to do and there are no lines or boundaries, they'll press ahead as fools.

INSANE MESSAGES OF FEMINISTS

It's the opposite message to what your daughters should know. The abortion culture is horrible.

LIBERAL WITCHES

Big butts and breasts: everything is caricatured and superficial for sure. Be sweet and mature!

Modern women are what these young men have to deal with. Don't tell em to go with older, this is it.

I think it's rampant easy sex that creates mental illness. In fact from my research I am sure of it.

Not only promiscuous sex but bisexual sex, why not? In immoral societies it happens when drunk.

DIONYSIAN MAD MAX

This Dionysian mad max scenario builds up inside to create a hall of demons and madness, aye.

Without lines people lose their minds. Bisexual, gay, group sex, triangles even animals=hell ties.

This is the insane setting kids are presented with and they're encouraged in it too don't forget.

Sin creates SYMPTOMS, a fact recorded by William James in his book on repentance/religion.

Sin creates symptoms and repentance brings wellness again. Hmmm--think there's a connection?

The Golden Girls in the nineties normalized, justified and even superiorized sex, it was the main focus.

GOLDEN GIRLS: OLD SLUTS

Suddenly women were emulating Blanch the Slut. Thinking it was cute and not too much.

Two and 1/2 Men justified a whoremonger making him look dashing, rich, winning, a real looker.

LIBERAL WITCHES

In both sitcoms they were RICH, a profound message to the masses who emulate what they see, ouch.

Suddenly men were whoremongering thinking it was great & looking at women as meat/with hate.

It's a planned subversion of western culture by disrupting the sexes and the family for sure.

They have friend groups making themselves feel better than they actually are--maintaining the war.

They have friends to make themselves feel better than they actually are--maintaining the war.

HER GIRLFRIENDS COME FIRST

If she goes for a real man her girlfriends get triggered and "concerned" and with trouble, she turns.

They're delusional about themselves: "you gotta earn it". They bought that they're valuable/entitled.

Disgusting vanity is reinforced by a hundred men after them online whenever showing their face.

They don't see how stupid they look. They don't know history, answer foolishly, never read a book.

She drinks daily not just on weekends, and her answer is "I'm young, I do what I want with friends".

As men get sweeter and more conciliatory the women take over more while being inferior see.

They aren't sexy, they're gross and repulsive but that's what the boys have to work with, witches.

No one--neither guys or girlfriends--will tell them this. There's no reality testing or its dismissed.

LIBERAL WITCHES

They hate truth tellers, recall how women have TDS so bad even Trump's name makes em crazy/sad.

They can't respect themselves, its impossible. So as they disrespect others they go down together.

It's sad to see a girl with much potential taking that route. Destiny disrupted/growth stunted, ouch.

The babyboomers were sick but each generation gets worse. Forget exceptions, it's a bellshaped curve.

RAMPANT FEMALE SEX SIN

Many therapists don't see it's a moral revolution we need in this country or hell's coming see.

Rampant sex sin in women means dirty sluts. Don't be afraid, speak on saving grace & mercy of God.

A repentant female may have self-forgiven but is still haunted by images cuz she sees the rotten.

Don't have sex with men and save yourself for a husband. Clear out the past and be awesome.

All you can think is: dam, what could have been! Now she's filled with tattoos & swears a lot too.

They think people see them as they always are, not unstable and changeable, ugly, not a star.

WHAT MADE EM WITCHES

TRAUMA BONDING

He triggers jealousy to control. Once you see that you never go back cuz this crap is getting old.

Any type of trauma bonding leaves one feeling very self-limited and I for one am done with it.

An ongoing toxic relationship with a hypercontrolling master manipulator was all I knew then sir.

As time passes the recipient becomes weaker and weaker as the giver is more evil as a faker.

GRINDING HER DOWN

Either he's a player who doesn't care or he's trying to make her jealous with constant triggers

He grinds her down so she has no self as he fills her with him and his guff on the way to hell.

The narcissist demands subjugation maintained by the other thinking she's the impossible one.

What happens to a decent person when trauma bonded to a malignant narcissist? Bedlam

Nothing ever satisfied him. I had to become a yes person to avoid his wrath. Recovered woman

A trauma bond means a sick stomach and constant anxiety and I for one thank God it's history.

"It was lots of verbal abuse and constant shame, calling me names". Totally recovered lady

WHAT MADE EM WITCHES

When he thrills you with adrenalin turn it around cuz it's all fear and it's killing you ma'am.

He kills you with adrenalin by his constant comparisons and making you feel less than.

One way or another he gets his zingers in there to make you feel vulnerable, small, uglier.

THE SICKENING SYSTEM

I had to comply and I hated it. My worth and self-respect weren't just stolen but trampled upon.

Remnants: To this day I struggle with self-doubt. It compels constant improvement, wow.

Ceaseless fear and profound grief: these are the words of those who've been in trauma bonds see.

Survivor: I feel like damaged goods--will I ever feel acceptable or lovable? Brain trouble

I felt so alone. I was always told if I left I'd die. A huge psychotic spell developed 'til rescue, aye.

He actually thinks it's reasonable to grind you into the ground. Every message brings you down.

You had so many experiences of being robbed of your own decency that you accepted dregs see.

Having held a torch for my rejector all my life there was a strange & peculiar relief when he died.

It was a mental and spiritual drought living in a small liberal town but now I feel free, sovereign.

CONSTANT TRIGGERS OF ANXIETY

WHAT MADE EM WITCHES

Every time you talk to him you feel anxiety. He's controlling your mind/self-image honey.

Go no contact and never go to his channel. You can rise again by releasing this hypnotic spell.

His power is in keeping you DOWN: focused on him, the giver of grief like you've never known.

Once free of this crud, see it not as waste but the lesson of deep wisdom and also lucrative.

PERVERTED MALE CULTURE UNDERTOW

There isn't a woman alive who hasn't experienced degradation as the world breaks her down.

A refugee of a narc system has it inscribed in her DNA: no more abuse and a queen for *every* day.

After I let him into my house and he ruined my life, who's to blame for that? Me principally, aye.

It's a wasted life angry at an assailant you let into your house. You even wanted him there at first!

This isn't the fifties when you could trust your first date. Give up being nice, you could be raped.

If a man brings friends to your house he's a louse. It's rude, invasive and dangerous too no doubt.

ELDERING IS AN *INNER* JOURNEY

Stop stuffing info and get into YOU since no one else will and life's too short for all that too.

Because I worked and waited, not pushing just to accomplish, it became far more creative.

LIBERAL WITCHES

When all your high school friends are dead what are you supposed to think? It's all groupthink

When older you should be eldering not declining. Saging not aging/work till you're dying.

You work and enjoy life until one day you're dead, that's all--not slow diminishment in hospitals.

In fifties eating a lump of butter on the vegetables enabled 24 hour fasting or at least no-snacking.

To be happy you know God's in control and that He rewards good and punishes bad/not you.

NOT A PERSON BUT AN ILLNESS

She wasn't a person but a mental illness profile and lower archetype while being in total denial.

Was she a dam slut or a scared little girl who knew no other way, who just caved in naturally?

Was she a slut or a traumatized woman who for pure survival had to be open/available to men?

Was she a slut or an incest victim who had no idea what she was doing just to avoid tragedy?

Was she a slut or an incest victim with no idea what she was doing just to avoid tragedy?

What 12 year old girl has the mental foundation to stand up for chastity let alone decency?

Caving into sex cures all ills and solves all riddles. It prevents being alone, a big fear of kids.

TRIGGERING MEMORIES

WHAT MADE EM WITCHES

The kind of sex demanded will prey on her conscience in older years and these images persevere.

Does it make sense to let old memories ruin your day, hour or minute? When it comes, BLOCK IT.

Be a 1950's woman, that's a good and safe archetype to follow and lasts through life/a perennial.

Women hated me, smear campaigners. They were always on the horn slandering: gossipers.

BE LIKE A JOCKEY

Regarding the body I'm like a jockey: I don't like non-essentiality or superfluity so it's gone today.

In fifties eating butter on the vegetables enabled 24 hour fasting or at least no-snacking.

They fire tucker just as Title 42 ends. It's gonna be an epic catastrophe so get ready friends.

Things are so dire and no one knows about it. News is an arm of Biden's dems who censor it.

THE END: COMPLETION

After writing 95,000 proverbs and 120 books I am exhausted/need rest. It was automatic I insist.

When done I looked around and saw God had already rewarded me! It's now--I have it all see.

Who goes to their office and looks at the view 8 hours a day? It is me: for writing it is the only way.

I did the best I know how, that's all I know. Now with completion I'll just relax/go with the flow.

LIBERAL WITCHES

FEMALE WITCHES ON THE WAY UP
NARCISSISM DEFINED BY JEALOUSY
NARCISSIST SMEAR CAMPAIGNS
SUFFERING SLIGHTEST OFFENSE
PLAYS THE VICTIM CARD
THE INABILITY TO REJECT LESS
THE POWER OF RELOCATION—GETTING AWAY
MENTAL ILLNESS IS MAL-ADAPTATION
WIVES MUST BE STRONG TOO
THE STRENGTH TO REJECT
POLITE CRUELTIES: AGEIST REMARKS
NO OPTION TO BE WEAK
CRYBABY ROUTINE
MAGNET TO PREDATORY MEN
DAILY INVALIDATION OF CHILDREN
RELIEVED OF WORTHLESS MYTH
EXPECT SUDDEN LIFE CHANGE!
GOD INPUTES UNEARNED SELF-WORTH
COMMON SHIT-TESTS
SMART WOMEN KNOW MEN
SIN: HOLES IN YOUR BUCKET
YOU CAN'T COME IN TO CHARGE PHONE!
BLENDED FAMILIES
BROKEN FAMILY ENTANGLEMENTS
LET YOUR LIFE SWING FORWARD
SEX EXPLOITATION BY WOMEN
HEDGE OF PROTECTION GOES DOWN
WITCH TYRANTS
THE RELEASE OF CRIMINALS IS FASHIONABLE
BORDERS MOST IMPORTANT
A GENERATION WITHOUT HOBBIES OR PROJECTS
SOCIAL IS THE WHOLE THING
ONLY BY BEING IMPOSED ON CONSTANTLY

LIBERAL WITCHES

LOSING AMERICA TO POCS GOING DEMOCRAT
VIOLENCE AND GUNS [SELF-DEFENSE]
SOCIAL HYPNOTISM MAINTAINS LIBERAL NARRATIVE
NO SOLITUDE IN LIBERAL TOWNS
PUT DOWN FOR BEING ANTI-SOCIA
PEOPLE YEARS ARE BAD MEMORIES, SOLITUDE IS LUXURY
OPEN BORDERS IN THE HOME: HORRORS!
GUN CONTROL NEVER ENDS ONCE IT STARTS
SOCIAL PSYCHOLOGY IS NOT LIKE THIS
ENANTIODROMIA: OPPOSITES
GOD WANTS A STABLE MATE FOR YOU
WOMEN CONTROLLING MEN THRU SEX
YOUR DIVINE TURF OR SANCTUARY
YOUR SERENITY BRINGS FLIP-FLOPS
YOUR WORK IS GOD'S FOR THIS TIME
THE PATH TO GENIUS: FORGET IT
DON'T LET THEM IN!
OSTRACIZNG
YOU'RE NOT GOOD IF YOU SLEEP AROUND
INTERPERSONAL DISSONANCE IS PAIN
VALUE OF LEISURE VS. TOO MUCH WORK
MORALITY LEARNED THE HARD WAY
NOT BORN THAT WAY
MARRIAGE IS A FENCE, AT LAST
KEEP SWEET AND HE'LL PROTECT YOUR RETREAT
SIN: TRASH BIN RUINED YOUR KIN
GRANDMA: JUSTIFYING SIN IS NOT LOVIN'
BLESSED SEED AND GENIUS CHRISTIANS
CHANGE OF SEASONS
GOD HAS TO RELEASE IT
DIETARY THOUGHTS ON AUTOIMMUNITY
NEW DIET THOUGHTS: JUICE/BEANS/RICE
FATS CREATE WRINKLES
FRUIT MAKES US CUTE

LIBERAL WITCHES

You have little men and you have little petty women. On the way up that's what you gotta deal with.

FEMALE WITCHES ON THE WAY UP

She shows her ruthless bulliness whenever she gets an edge and then you wish you were dead.

Satan is jealous, it's the devil in all of us. But life is hell when faced with it especially in feminists.

They target scapegoat and won't let go their entire life. Even after death some grudges remain, aye.

Instantly the women sized me up and squeezed me out. "Have nothing to do with her" they mocked.

You hear of older sister wives beating the younger ones up. It's women so how could we doubt it.

Shock: The female narcissist has designs on the husband in order to move the woman out.

NARCISSISM DEFINED BY JEALOUSY

She's just jealous of what you have and the closest route is her own body used as barter.

Don't let her around your husband for a female narcissist has no morals/can't trust em.

LIBERAL WITCHES

First thing she's thinking is: Hmmm, how do I move her out and myself in? Through HIM."

It's a desolate land if you settle for less having friends like this but that's the female community sis.

Yes a Jezebel can take down a man but taking down various women is much more often.

About human enmity, hear: Just because she's a looker from the cosmetic counter they hate her.

She shines/will pay for being great in any way. That's the way it is in the female community.

You were unequally hooked to that Jezebel just cuz she was meaner and a schemer/you feared her.

God gave you escape outa Dodge. Now don't bring Dodge with you and all will be as promised.

NARCISSIST SMEAR CAMPAIGNS

For narcissists are schemers and smear campaigners. They are truce breakers and life ruiners.

They move in swarms called flying monkeys. You can be rid of this web in a minute by moving away.

I still shudder at the memory of the crap they put me thru. A swarm of invaders, feeling entitled too.

A narcissist learns early that being honest and forthright is way too risky so they hide it see.

They are beyond sneaky drama seekers steeped in jealousy even ruining one in own family.

Due to pathological envy the female narcissist can be incredibly cruel thinking nothing of it.

LIBERAL WITCHES

If she gets her sights on you get ready for a bumpy ride. Real or perceived, you're the despised.

Real or perceived, anything she's jealous of consigns you to hell on earth for awhile love.

The female family narcissist is a trouble maker, driven by desperate need of supply of whatever.

She loves making people feel beneath her, obligated to her, insecure because of her, low tier.

Feeling superior is supply to her, and when injured someone has to pay, usually a family member.

In her mind she has been slighted, devalued or unappreciated in some way/someone must pay.

SUFFERING SLIGHTEST OFFENSE

Real or imaginary, all narcissists can suffer the slightest offense and the backlash is ruthless.

Were you exposed to jealousy/hatred as a little girl? Despite no memory this was your whole world.

If you don't realize you're dealing with one who is jealous and you're being devalued, life is hell.

Your early life was hell for no other reason than a monster was jealous and envious, think of that.

If as a child you can't understand this, the monster has devastating effects on your self-worth sis.

Your therapy is understanding it had nothing to do with you, just another jealousy-driven shrew.

Repeatedly makes you feel bad about yourself, stupid, unwelcome or a dam embarrassment.

LIBERAL WITCHES

It has nothing to do with you/everything to do with her consumed and motivated by jealousy/envy.

She's brilliant at triangulating other family members against each other--it's like a superpower.

She must be treated by all as if superior to everyone else. She knows better, leading us out.

These women give high maintenance a whole new meaning. They create catastrophes usually.

The opinion leader is also the serial bully in the family, acting as the thought police or censuring.

The only logical reaction is to view every interaction with her as a calculated set-up and never trust.

PLAYS THE VICTIM CARD

If the female narcissist doesn't get her way she'll flip into being victim. That's her go-to ma'am.

She's highly successful at garnering pity and sympathy for her plight casting you as villain, aye.

There's no level they won't exploit and these women fight DIRTY. Come hell it's all about WINNING.

It's near impossible to admit we have a monster in our own family, cognitive dissonance is blinding.

If you have such a woman in your family she's gonna be trouble, period. Accept this, it's serious. START

Relentless targeting due to envy/jealousy is the opposite to Christianity--the devil in families.

She's not gonna see the light, you can't have hearty conversations with her, give up the fight.

LIBERAL WITCHES

Admit it then get on with your life. Use grey rock--ignore this human being day and night.

You must deprive them of the narcissistic supply they get from abusing you. Separate, move.

A narcissistic parent sets one up for a lifetime of making excuses for people's bad behavior.

The narcissist's victim invalidates herself and lives with anxiety, guilt and shame her whole lifetime.

it sets one up for trauma-bonded relationships in adulthood or enablers who misunderstood.

DAILY INVALIDATION OF CHILDREN

A narc parent is a special kind of hell: decades of daily invalidation, meanness and pettiness.

Emotional manipulation, affection withholding, comparing and gaslighting is soul-killing.

Gaslighting a child: "Don't be so sensitive" or "that never happened" or "I didn't mean that".

Mother's insanity is not your fault but every abused child thinks it is. If only that, if only this.

Victim anxiety: You may not be at peace until they have passed and many suffer long after that.

The monkey on your back--old voices, invalidations, nastiness--may not end when they die: fact.

There is a prevailing relief when a narcissistic parent passes but it's accompanied with guilt sis.

Do grief work in complex losses to help you process it so you can just go on, disentrenched.

LIBERAL WITCHES

Step away from family enablers too and prune your family tree. They justified the problem see.

He's of the world, boring. Making pointless points about nothing, come on. Get a life, so long.

Don't let it go to your head for it's easy come easy go. Gov can strip you of everything even now.

RELIEVED OF WORTHLESS MYTH

It's relieving to recognize that feelings of worthlessness and guilt are symptoms of depression, not true reality.

It's total relief beyond measure to realize you're NOT worthless--it's just a symptom as the brain depresses.

Feeling worthless, guilty and ashamed then to realize it's not true/has no baring, it's just depression and you're ok.

Realizations that depression actually causes you to have low opinions of yourself broke me thru to the magic elf.

Though it held me back, I was hidden. Not the Dunning-Kruger Effect of a dummy broadcasting stupid visions.

I have seen people change so fast with just this knowledge--by painful symptoms they're no longer held hostage.

Getting past depression-based worthlessness is so important as life decisions are made and all of life is changed.

EXPECT SUDDEN LIFE CHANGE

Getting past depression-based worthlessness is important as life decisions are made drastically changing our fate.

Decisions as to who we let into our life and who we let go--changes our fate suddenly/maybe from hell below.

LIBERAL WITCHES

If I feel worthless, it must be because I AM worthless—that's how we think. Seeing the falsehood brings RELIEF.

Guilt and shame: always reliving history and shuddering! That's depression, you should have good memories.

Seeing ourselves as all sinners but owned by God as winners in unearned victory as His sons and daughters.

THE INABILITY TO REJECT LESS

Better to be alone than locked up with some man who doesn't bring to the table what you deserve.

Your inability to reject less: See you gotta be willing to turn stuff away not take the first guy ok.

You must Create a Space to be ready for what God really has for you not let clowns in too.

Stop saying yes to everything ["no"-averse] and urgently start calibrating your priorities first.

All I had was a lot of energy, drive and will power. I repented of sin so anticipated God's favor.

THE POWER OF RELOCATION—GETTING AWAY

You have power over him just by moving away since his power came from bothering you all day.

God didn't bring me my soul mate until I showed Him I was capable of rejecting less. R.C. Blakes

When you start accepting less than you deserve the world will bring you lower and lower girl.

You have a breakup + you get drunk + more bad stuff until you spiral down + you've bottom out.

LIBERAL WITCHES

The solution is to never accept anything less--not an inch. You gotta be strong to be staunch.

Especially if you're a woman, life will be hard, rough and humiliating falling to lower levels: be ready.

Men will catch you in lower webs and expect perversions instead: you'll wanna be dead.

Never feel inferior being older regarding finding a partner. Sexual Market Value [SMV] is bull sir.

Older men want established women of substance they can relate to and young men love us too.

Never ever miss someone or think you need him. What are you, an appendage? Do YOUR thing.

An obsessive longing or falling in love overnight is a trauma bond made worse by getting tight.

The inability to reject less than I deserve is an invitation to self-abuse. We must discern, vet, choose.

MENTAL ILLNESS IS MAL-ADAPTATION

Any mental illness I incurred came by mal-adapting to liberals in my environment or over me.

Especially as a woman. When you start looking at your age and devaluing yourself it's over man.

When things aren't right you must articulate it. Don't keep settling and lowering tho' you hate it.

If my articulating truth is going to drive you away it means our season together is over anyway.

Strength is our only option. To entertain ideas of weakness [peace at any price] is self-sabotage.

LIBERAL WITCHES

A woman can't afford to be weak. The world doesn't give her that option lest she's overcome see.

WIVES MUST BE STRONG TOO

Tho' God blesses with a husband the world is so vicious surging in you gotta be strong against sin.

I was so weak when the world surged in I went into denial and blunted my feelings to get thru it.

When husband left I was thrown to the wolves. I had no defense or assertion against the tidal waves.

Visit the rich widow cuz the world flows in to separate her from her money and she's all alone.

THE STRENGTH TO REJECT

Strength to reject: whether you're single or with husband elect. Strength blocks the world's hex.

Don't you dare ask me for money. I don't even want your company now go away you phony.

Yah they all wanna help, for a price. Mainly to worm their way into your house, a gossiping mouse.

You gotta be strong against housekeepers. They too are looking to overtake you the jealous upstarts.

Be strong against their polite cruelties and subtle remarks to bring the queen down: hark!

POLITE CRUELTIES: AGEIST REMARKS

Jealousy. They immediately think: how can I bring her down and move myself in? Women = envyin'

Young housekeepers making sly remarks about age to undercut the Queen, a sage. Fire the page.

LIBERAL WITCHES

Ageist remarks are **NOT** subtle, **VERY** intentional and cruel. Know that, fire the fool, resume cool.

Young maids singing songs about the old bag to undercut the queen: It's obvious see.

Now listen: you can't even **THINK** weakness or your whole world will cave in tho' you're rich.

They're jealous, they don't wanna clean your house. Who are you they think and there it starts.

You gotta be strong, you can't always work thru a foreman. All animals sense weakness man.

I was so miserable with housekeepers in my house. That's my environment, my niche you grouch.

I finally saw then I couldn't afford to be weak cuz it makes one miserable day from stupidity.

They'd butter up my husband and make remarks about him. They'd ask me personal questions.

NO OPTION TO BE WEAK

You don't have an option to be weak cuz they'll kill you. Strength is your only option I'm telling you.

The worst were the "welcoming dinners" where they'd insult me all thru them the jealous vixens.

Dogs can smell fear–the world smells weakness! Then life can become a mess very fast miss.

A woman must walk strong yet that doesn't mean masculine but self-certitude and confident.

Even if private life is unraveling you don't broadcast that or air your dirty laundry in public darling.

LIBERAL WITCHES

I was so maudlin I guess it was a cry for attention. A cry for help actually since inside I was crumblin'

CRYBABY ROUTINE

The crybaby routine gets you nowhere fast. Give that up for the highest: taking dominion at last.

No matter who you were it's now that matters, and they can't see both sides simultaneously sir.

Ageism is defeatism as the world flows in to remind you having no other way to put you down.

You've perfected. Unable to find a flaw they'll always pull the age card so be strong against it.

In an ageist culture "old man/old woman" is a put down. We must see the cruel signs all around.

Everything's in reverse. You can't show weakness as a woman as predatory men sniff it out fast.

Weak men are bullied but weak women are raped, robbed, moved in on, used and mobbed.

MAGNET TO PREDATORY MEN

Instantly you have predatory men at your front door manipulating you with your own mindset.

You can be taken in by teen age boys, your own son or all his friends. Get a grip/get strong woman!

There are even weak women sleeping with their son's friends. That's how lowdown weakness is.

Weakness will take you down the rabbit hole as you spiral down to hell. It's a pull as you fall.

LIBERAL WITCHES

As you get weaker you need your evil associates more esp. as your real friends depart in horror.

I hope you can see the necessity of being strong. Learn the lessons I endured being pulled down.

Weakness dissolves your morals and boundaries too. Soon you're crying out for foes to protect you.

If faint in the day of adversity your strength is small. In your inner constitution there's work to do.

I lived in a tiny dusty cabin to see how the world mistreats through predatory projections.

You must grow from inside out as a woman. Every little test, "oh" but there's no safety net now.

GOD INPUTES UNEARNED SELF-WORTH

It's not me that earns the self-worth but owned by God He moves me to do good works raising it first.

Stop bemoaning the past cuz the bad was a necessary part of the hero's journey--it's archetypal all thru history

In a depressed state she decides to leave her husband, abandon her dog, major things like that--bad!

Now that you see your feelings of worthlessness are unreal you can pursue your talents with great appeal.

I can't report on Kamala cuz I can't stand to watch her. Everything's in reverse like she's SO superior.

Even tho' you were "unaware" of what you were doing I'm sure you enjoyed doing it cuz inside is a sadist.

You think you're opaque but buddy I can see right thru you and I don't like what I see: a narcissist and fake.

LIBERAL WITCHES

You think a smart woman doesn't know men like you? It's our responsibility to give this wisdom to the youth.

Fruit at night is no good. It ferments the starch lunch--I'd stick to skipping dinner/starting with fruit juice.

God took me from a penthouse driving a Jaguar to a shack in the desert with no car so be very cautious dear.

Give people NO control over your feelings, your words, what you want/wish for yourself and above all your time.

COMMON SHIT-TESTS

Men know women be envyin' so that's how they shit test em: talk about the beauty of ANY other woman.

It has to do with sex and violence as bad as it gets. I just wanna peaceful life of love if only just for pets.

If a woman's been thru a lot--seasons of shit tests and rot--she's not gonna go along with this so listen up.

It's my beautiful home and thoughts and the rest of this lovely day and then the night behind a locked gate.

For the FIRST time no one's imposing on me so I'm sure not gonna let you do it anymore buddy: emotionally.

A smart women isn't just reacting to words but WORLDS of meaning behind em/suddenly the thrill is gone.

YOU HURT ME. That's all I know or need to know. Be like the hillbilly in Andy of Mayberry: 3 words that's all.

He tortures me with my own emotions--that's what's wrong with him. Unhappy lady in therapy

SMART WOMEN KNOW MEN

LIBERAL WITCHES

Any woman with smarts has had it with men like you. She knows the signs and symbols making us blue.

Pastor came by and gave my land a spring cleaning! Looks so palatial and majestic I can't even believe it.

We create through ELIMINATION. I didn't "give" all the wood to the neighbors they relieved me of the clutter.

It helps immensely to know it was God's punishment thru people, not them. This lessens resentments ma'am.

When you act right this kinda crap isn't happening. God punishes evil/rewards good and that makes us happy.

When in sin we stir powers of darkness thru people but with repentance God turns His wrath on them for real.

After tyranny I'm as humble as can be and hate seeing what's happening to my country so Lord, please use me!

Kamala: Major-taxer and military-slasher. She's also a big JAILER of anyone with a different narrative.

SIN: HOLES IN YOUR BUCKET

SIN: troubles, holes in your bucket, wrath, calumny, envy. REPENT: happiness, influence, success, bounty.

I guess that's what I get for wishful thinking--shoulda never let you enter my door. Rhianna: Rehab

If too far-fetched they don't get it. But you being egotistic assume they do since YOU understand it.

A writer simply must get to that point of humility where they GET it independent of whether HE gets it.

If your stuff is too dam far-fetched and silly it's not even funny it's an embarrassment so shut up buddy.

LIBERAL WITCHES

You can't get to the high station as a writer cuz your **EGO** is all I hear and a definite block calling yourself a seer.

I just don't give a dam. I've dialed up what's intolerable to me now and I've decided you're not worth my time.

I am not gonna listen to your longwinded explanations of things that don't really matter, good bye dear.

I'm sick of going thru changes cuza you: up and down and things I didn't plan--you're a roller coaster man.

When love is like a roller coaster up and down it's not for me or anyone who wants to create/make good actions.

See true reality, not what he says it is. Have your version, take no account of egotistic perceptions.

Kamala was the leader of a liberal mob trying to destroy a good and decent man, over and again.

He doesn't have the intelligence indicating what **DOESN'T** belong--lacking that he lives in chaos all day long.

You get up too late then it's too hot to work. What a jerk--not the American work ethic but a curse.

You don't need those characters--caricatures of what humans are to look like, comical figures.

YOU CAN'T COME IN TO CHARGE PHONE!

Don't **ALLOW** disrespect to your privacy by them using you as a charging station for their phone--go home.

You're not a bus station or a place to deposit their friends--as if you mix with anyone/everyone for their benefit.

People will use every bit of you unless you draw **LINES**. The more you give in the more they'll destroy your mind.

LIBERAL WITCHES

I gave you a plot on the land for trailer hook up for your "solitude" but you spent all your time with me dude.

Every time someone stayed they ruined our life. Or any third party and the system was filled with strife.

When a man's depedestalized it can be a terrible and haunting thing. She backed him and now he's empty.

So now when you feel guilty/worthless you know what to confess: this is JUST because I am depressed.

Just once, be your own therapist/best friend and administer to your core self to release that man.

BLENDED FAMILIES

In the evil land we are ruled by CHILDREN and there's nothing more ruthless as in ALL wars by men.

When ruled by children I was apprehensive all the time day and night. So unpredictable but darkness, lies.

Just having em in the house/having to adapt made me terrified/sick as hell-- they're in control, that's all.

Teen stepchildren for example--there's a sweet dynamic there. No matter her role she's without a prayer.

It was an atom bomb: the twisted dynamics in blended families of triangulation and it's histrionics.

In this war zone, affairs can happen--a misguided device to switch the hate and violence to love and comfort.

BROKEN FAMILY ENTANGLEMENTS

When her stepson said he DESPISED her she couldn't take it and initiated their affair--it's very common dear.

LIBERAL WITCHES

And to think I was **LIVING** with em. I was in my twenties and a basketcase of mal-adaptations without wisdom.

There's nothing like a happy home of friendly brethren and wisdom is knowing how fast you can lose it ma'am.

So I gave em a plot for their solitude and they spent **ALL** their time at my pad and I allowed it being mad.

They wanna partake in my solitude way out here so they come over and **RUIN** it forever, human clutter.

They're empty inside/terrified of being alone, defined by society. So they cling, bother, interrupt, get bitchy.

They get **RESTLESS** and start to cause trouble some way. Pull you down, interrupt, change plans suddenly.

In a "secure functioning" relationship we're fully integrated with our own thoughts/feelings not divorced from them.

We choose him with our eyes, jam in qualities we'd like him to have then suffer when he lacks. Susan Winter

Make peace with it: **THIS** is the ride. Until you accept or reject it you're gonna be in torture with this guy.

Inconsistency is the major red flag with a partner who either doesn't want it or doesn't want it with you.

Can you see him as an occasional treat? That means to depedestalize him too for his inevitable cheat.

LET YOUR LIFE SWING FORWARD

Only one answer: let your own life swing forward as your **ALL** just as you allow his image to fade/vaporize/fall.

Inconsistency is the major red flag with a partner who either doesn't want it or doesn't want it with you.

LIBERAL WITCHES

This is to inoculate you to the crap she's sayin'. Everything's in reverse, it's very frustrating.

I'm glued to the tube to hear comments. This is history happening as we fall into the abyss.

With overwhelming stress and trauma the personality can fragment under the pressure: decompensation.

He just doesn't have the skill set for a relationship honey. It's like asking a legless man to run a race to victory.

Once Trump's gone and we're in the WH we'll come for his supporters next for you betrayed us. Kamala Harris

The left loves the dictator of China where they killed 150 million people. The left is despicably evil.

Ignoring scientific facts and putting left wing politics ahead of reality--we're in big trouble/it's gonna be tragic.

SEX EXPLOITATION BY WOMEN

You're like Willy Brown known for womanizing and influence-peddling and you seem proud of that buddy.

You're like Willie Brown known for womanizing and influence-peddling and you seem proud of that buddy.

Sex exploitation of men is the female side of sexual harassment and Kamala's the poster girl for it.

Sexual harassment is a criminal form of gender discrimination outlawed in California but NOT when against men?

Harassment is from man to woman but sex exploitation is when women use sex to move up in the ranks.

Sex harassment/exploitation warps workplace cultures and I recall it with a shudder/wouldn't wanna be younger.

LIBERAL WITCHES

Like many, Kamala saw sex exploitation as a way to jump the queue for career advancement and influence.

Female sex privilege creates a world where good girls don't get a chance-- sexual fascism by a glance.

HEDGE OF PROTECTION GOES DOWN

Any new girl in town, block or office is targeted with jealous ridicule and women are getting pugnacious too.

To create a family, sex must be valuable. But sex is NOT valuable in a promiscuous culture or model.

Kamala wants us to have NO police and NO self-defense as well. That doesn't work and it sounds like hell.

How to keep a happy home: don't let anyone else in. I've learned this after a lifetime of feeling imposed on.

A commie dictator like Kamala would tell me I gotta have five families in my house, not just me like it is now.

When God removes your hedge of protection your life goes from happy to blue instantly as evil flows in.

I didn't get the hedge back until I got married and even then we had to overcome problems with third parties.

Every time I let someone in they ruin my life. NOT HAPPENING again, I deserve my life of paradise.

You're not getting into Paradise cuz you'll bring your friends, evil gossip, stupid advice and smell like fish.

I'm not gonna go for a one-shot deal or an occasional treat. I want a life partner not a vacillator/micro-cheat.

WITCH TYRANTS

LIBERAL WITCHES

The witch tyrants are horrible cuz it's the maternal instinct reversed: pray for the adorable.

Psychological reversals evince both extremes: From most tender to most weird and mean.

The Social Throng: Needing constant attention so they can feel better about being wrong.

It's just a buncha no-good people worshipping themselves so I won't be there, thanks.

Victimhood is a way of seducing people, getting them all riled up and involved and it's evil.

These godless women support abortion/same sex marriage and they hate God, men and family.

Jezebel Spirit: Whatever axe they have to grind with you they'll have their guys do the dirty work.

THE RELEASE OF CRIMINALS IS FASHIONABLE

The release of criminals is very fashionable. The left wants everything opposite to reasonable.

But is releasing criminals merciful? Leftists don't care about that just a false ideology fulfilled.

Stay MINDFUL: keep bringing it back to your breathing {THE PRESENT} instead of the hateful.

Dems manufacture: El Paso was a Hispanic dem tied to ANIFA and Ohio shooter a leftist loon.

Three mass shootings--Texas, Ohio, Oregon--in one day begins the Civil War: entree.

How could they think these things? Well they had it in the schools then it just increased.

LIBERAL WITCHES

Jezebel Warning: The MINUTE she gets an edge she'll take over despite your distress.

BORDERS MOST IMPORTANT

I speak as someone who lived without a wall around my house in a small town without cops.

Life is evolution: you were weak back then so evil flowed in, now you're strong so forget it man.

Those zombie robots are ruled by instinct not reason so SEE that then let it all go--move on!

Of course they're gonna rob you if you're weak: Know these freaks then move on, relieved.

Not "how could he do this to me?" but "why did I let evil in and what does it say about ME?

Even if they weren't evil, you didn't know about these people before you let em in--stupid!

I was so naive, sheltered, stupid and weak I actually thought all people were nice or just geeks.

A GENERATION WITHOUT HOBBIES OR PROJECTS

A generation without hobbies or projects like a geek-they got sidetracked by sex, even preteen.

I relate to Blanche in Streetcar: The fine being imposed on by big/denser tho' less is more.

Like puppies/kittens imposed on constantly, can't the ramshackle sick world just let em be?

Since WWII, SOCIAL has replaced INDEPENDENCE as the highest priority and oh what a tragedy.

LIBERAL WITCHES

NOT true genius: Stilted, stupid utterances to "fit" the social world, terrified of disapproval.

I won't say I'm holy blameless but I've repented of my sins and swept out my closet of skeletons.

Not sure what it was but something scared me half to death and it was the declining culture itself.

My peers were from messy homes and I was scared cuz Mom kept things nice like Rome.

But there were other unnerving weird things about em cuz licentious sex sins was predominatin'

They didn't care about a thing, there were no lines and they were callous: my peers were a mess.

I couldn't stand my peers and would do anything to miss school where there were bullies too.

SOCIAL IS THE WHOLE THING

When the Jezebel gets jealous then she'll get her army against you, I promise--watch this.

They would bully me cuz I wasn't social and never wanted to leave home. Lord, please come!

At home it's fascination, inspiration, otherworldly elaboration but the social is BORING!

Why would I wanna twiddle my thumbs with zombies when solitude makes me so happy and free?

The more solitude I had the more interesting i was to them as escape, but that's my bad fate.

You think I'd talk to you again after your cruel zinger the last time? You missed your chance man.

LIBERAL WITCHES

Anorexia is an emotional illness--they are rare. It's a bottomless empty pit wanting her Lord.

He rejected Jesus and became a pagan. Tho' he seemed nice I was inwardly frightened of him.

The male feminist is so screwed up he becomes a sadist instead and I've experienced it: sad.

The more solitude the less I could forebear social intricacies, duplicities and phony sillies.

The anorexic will do anything to carve out her own domain amidst the total chaos of the insane.

Anti-white laws go under the innocent sounding name of "Affirmative Action".

It hurts to misfit: a major obstacle the overcoming of which brings genius to success, not death.

ONLY BY BEING IMPOSED ON CONSTANTLY

Only by being imposed on constantly could I learn the importance of solitude and boundaries.

Being without puts you at the mercy of others or as slaves to a dying social system.

Dependency on others whether for rides or whatever makes you their slave unless you clever.

"Classes" on homosexuality are no more than campaigns for immorality.

Whites aren't doing the killing, they kill 45% and are 60% of pop, blacks kill 50% and are 13% of pop.

Tech giants: no borders, nations or local religions; nothing against Big Pharma, Agra or Medicine.

LOSING AMERICA TO POCS GOING DEMOCRAT

LIBERAL WITCHES

If we lose America to the people of color they'll all go democrat and the USA will be over.

They're coming from hell holes to our beautiful country America to create hell holes.

They keep voting them in cuz they're black, and the blacks hate the whites: fact.

And a politician has to do is shout "racism" and blacks go into a trance, voting em in again.

Black hucksters feel no pressure to do right knowing they'll be voted in until they die.

Boys raised by women filling their heads with this crap cowtow to their wives and lose love fast.

Beta male vs dominatrix: She wants to get away and he begs her to stay crying like a baby.

God wanted me to write about feminism so He gave me a mother and two older sisters into it.

As our society becomes less moral we've seen an escalation of violence in the country.

I detest gatherings/groups--an inundation of snippy thoughts as they all wanna know the scoop.

VIOLENCE AND GUNS [SELF-DEFENSE]

With tragic violence the calls to give up freedoms in exchange for security become deafening.

Terrorism is manufactured to try to sell you tyranny in the form of "security", see?

Taking our 2nd Amendment rights is no solution it just takes the guns of law-abiding citizens.

LIBERAL WITCHES

El Paso shooter picked a gun-free zone for a reason but bad guys will always have guns.

Logic doesn't work with authoritarians they just want gov to do something by taking freedoms.

Chicago has the hardest gun laws in the country but they have the most gun deaths--see?

Why not fix their own country NOT bringing their immorality and lack of standards here?

Most are angry black women raising boys to be just like them but beta males can be violent.

All angry people feel like victims and they blame someone else for that, ridiculous.

Feminists think it's great women are raising their sons to be like them but it's not, it's lame.

CHAOS without the natural order of God over man, man over woman, woman over children.

SOCIAL HYPNOTISM MAINTAINS LIBERAL NARRATIVE

The fact they're so dumb puts you way ahead so stop being mad at the brainless hypnotized left.

They're all idiots and you know it. My only hope is for one sane one in the clan but I doubt it.

For social hypnotism is a narrative: One learned by rote and enforced by rejection threats.

So we're spreading stories creating hate and violence--cuz they don't believe em by chance?

They want racism to exist so by anecdotes alone they won't let it die or make it up to be pissed.

LIBERAL WITCHES

If upon unwanted interruption you lose an insight trust God will bring it back if He wants it.

I had to work it all out in Borrego Springs and it was hell on hot earth--125 degrees, cursed.

A hangover is far worse in a hot desert especially if the mountains socially close you in.

In the middle of the mountains is this desert town where everyone knows everything, oh.

I couldn't get isolated enough in a "hot" social climate--life was about getting more private.

It was so aggravating (you can't imagine) that I escaped to the back of a ghost-town all alone.

Another thing you should know is how cruel women can be--not "good" tho' they claim to be.

Learning to navigate this social milieu was my Ph.D. in the streets about how social devices stink.

After just one year of that I was relieved to live in a tiny shack with no one but my cat.

Borrego architecture is homes without fences--so you gotta put up with people (forbearance).

Just like Paul I was happy in the lowest circumstances but to me it was like a golden palace.

NO SOLITUDE IN LIBERAL TOWNS

SOLITUDE in nature: There's nothing like it so I made best of all things and made a home of it.

The only problem was when people came without calling first--a total imposition which hurt.

LIBERAL WITCHES

The more solitude I had through the years the less I could forebear people who bored me to tears.

When people came they seemed grabby and mean and I wanted only to make them leave!

Then I'd return to my reverie in solitude and be SO happy: a pattern for years after tragedy.

If you're agreeing to social events when you don't wanna go, DON'T. Be free: stay at home.

If I'm apprehensive of gatherings then I'm not gonna go and stay home where I'm happy.

And just so I don't have to keep explaining I tell em once: I never wanna go, don't even ask.

Social occasions are CHORES. Vicious, tedious, irritating pin-cushions and I won't have em.

Groups: I can read all their thoughts and know which ones don't like me and I need this NOT.

Because no matter how good something is "out there" it's always far far better "in here" if clear.

PUT DOWN FOR BEING ANTI-SOCIAL

I was put down and assaulted all my life for not being social, connected, available to the rabble.

The "dark" women in spirit support abortion, transgender and whatever: horrors!

"Dark" women are worlds apart from pro-life women a man could love and start a family with.

They are for everything that's evil--they hate men. Pro-life women are opposite, encouragin'.

LIBERAL WITCHES

He went too far going out on a limb on an error but deception brings itself down with a trigger.

You keep thinking of the bad things you did cuz that's how Satan gets you, so memory: forbid.

What's bringing me to the apex of my talent and game is SOLITUDE, for once I can work all day.

They want no light in their darkness. Try to talk to them and they'll throw you out.

There are evil women and good women out there and the difference is like night and day.

The ME-TOO rallies are like a dark night, a nightmare. I don't believe men are harassing them, sir.

They're out there deceiving every man, woman and child playing the victim role-, so don't go.

Do NOT fall for what they say. These are wicked evil women vs the pro lifers: family, God, children.

Be sure to tell the people: There's no such thing as racism there's only good vs. evil.

They wanna seduce, emotionalize and brainwash you cuz once controlled they've got you.

When the shooting story is presented they always say "white male" but never black male.

PEOPLE YEARS ARE BAD MEMORIES, SOLITUDE IS LUXURY

Why is it I only remember the "people years" not the 17 of total solitude without those tears?

An ugly old man called Barrack Obama is sticking his chicken neck into things in America.

LIBERAL WITCHES

Not only are they uncontrolled sinners, the kids have no training in productive days ordered.

It's time for a music holiday I say. That means no more news for awhile so I can MAKE HAY.

It was horrible being involved with those kids before I knew people could be callous and cruel.

No control, ethics or morals, no goals, calling me old, no respect for and a blight on the household.

There's nothing elders can do but stay away from pre-convict boys whose moms made em that way.

One juvenile delinquent in his arrogance forbade me to bash Obama in my own residence!

The creepier they are the more they love Obama and wanna kill you for not going along with it.

OPEN BORDERS IN THE HOME: HORRORS!

Marriage is a woman's only protection so she can burgeon and without it she's had it man.

If you're like a limp noodle in establishing borders the world will flow in and YOUR life is over.

I learned about open borders by having my home life turned upside down by youth invaders.

Social behavior and respect for privacy has degraded for three generations and they're really nasty.

They don't even know what it means to have a home or how HOME LIFE can be hell or heaven.

A household should run like a swiss watch: exact routines for max efficiency are established.

LIBERAL WITCHES

It used to be churches were fun when they told the truth, now it's Trump who is so cool.

The churches have fallen! They're the ones approving of open borders and this invasion, friends.

PTSD: After being in safe surroundings for three years I still have people-imposing-on-me fears.

People impose on you insofar as YOU don't establish boundaries so tell yourself you're sorry.

GUN CONTROL NEVER ENDS ONCE IT STARTS

If second amendment is against tyrannical government, why should they regulate it?

Mass shootings are not from crazies but a deep state using military attacks to take our guns.

Once they start gun control it'll never stop as they get their gumption up then round us all up.

Start gun control and you see more manufactured shootings so they can FINISH their deadly goal.

You take our guns then what do we do with deadly home invaders armed with AK-47s?

Criminals will always have em, dumb-dumb! Most murders occur where they've banned the guns.

Marriage is woman's only protection so she can burgeon and without it she surely needs a gun.

SOCIAL PSYCHOLOGY IS NOT LIKE THIS

You take a class on Social Psychology and it's not gonna be anything like what I'm describing.

LIBERAL WITCHES

Tho' it's unrepentant sins triggering their abuse, you build strength in resistance and are less obtuse.

I will persevere, not falling back down to the masses again but stay pure/love God and go on ahead.

Ironically the problem is you're TOO much. You go right over them but God will have a hunch.

For to fall back down to the masses again is a very hard fall and it is cruel as hell.

The Fallen Hero Syndrome is when they KILL you after adoring you: the viciousness of people.

ENANTIODROMIA: OPPOSITES

It's called ENANTIODROMIA: Everything converting to it's opposite like the sinner-saint gestalt.

After that I am ever-ready/take nothing for granted cuz I know things can change in a minute.

Seeing people change like that--suddenly like in Nazi Germany--was a lesson in Social Psychology.

I take nothing or no one for granted with it comes to the human animal cuz we're also social.

The social brains mesh in circuity--it's called interactional synchrony so that's it for me.

No God doesn't want you to go for a ruffian 22 years younger who scares and "excites" you.

GOD WANTS A STABLE MATE FOR YOU

What God wants for you is a stable mate because of whom you're now flourishing top-rate.

LIBERAL WITCHES

So you were sick, so you were mentally ill/outa control, a real psychopath--now you're whole.

Your spirit attracted men back then who tore you down, used you and wasted your time.

WOMEN CONTROLLING MEN THRU SEX

What the women were like when I first moved to the desert was unbelievable, tragic, scary as hell.

It's like there's this huge unwritten pecking order so the new kid [girl] on the block faces horror.

White women "buy color" with guys: they pay for you to stay with them. Jesse Lee Peterson

Men are sex addicts and women are sex dealers. Jesse Lee Peterson

Emotionally addicted like any addict: Put her out and date her for a sexless year, you won't want her.

Women control men thru sex. It's like giving an addict free drugs but it comes with a Jezebel hex.

All she's doing is giving him what his ego needs so she control him without begging please.

It's a bartering system based on needs, wants and price payoff: this is not true love.

Just as drug dealer doesn't want addict to go free, she doesn't want to stop his sex spree.

We all start out wrong but once we see it why not straight away do things the right way?

Do right and live gets instantly better, take the wide road and it will never happen/you're a loser.

LIBERAL WITCHES

Liberals don't like the idea of an objective standard set by God, the Creator of all things.

Laws went from protecting the good FROM evil to supporting evil and to hell with the people.

They hate this president so much it's impossible to give him any credit for good, a bunch.

YOUR DIVINE TURF OR SANCTUARY

It helps to establish a home for yourself first in pristine beauty and routines, then invite him in.

If you're on YOUR turf he can't insult and if he does it's you who boots him out.

But wicked men wanna hypnotize weak women in their homes--win this war or be dumb.

Rule your domain and let no one call you "controlling"--he just wants to take over honey.

Or you can start by entering HIS world and it will be a whole other thing. Usually not for me.

For we're talking about ENVIRONMENT reflected in personality which is enhanced, or not.

If he loves your routines, selections and exquisite housekeepings then he may stay.

But when grossness enters in or he brings his buddies to be taking advantage again, ban him.

Worse thing about homelessness other than weather is the lack of protection against humans.

If sheltered from humans in your own unique paradise, you don't care what they think, aye?

LIBERAL WITCHES

He got arrogant and went too far out on a limb on an ERROR and that's how he's ruined, a failure.

I've done crazy things all from possession from substance or human spirits so I know it.

How much of your nagging guilt and shame is system-induced, have you thought of this today?

Because people control us by how they see us/peg us and we gotta stand up against this.

I'm going on ahead and never falling back for to do so would be hell on earth in fact.

YOUR SERENITY BRINGS FLIP-FLOPS

With his flip-flop or when his act is over, wow--your world implodes and you feel it's forever.

Just when you have happiness they get a little restless and trip you up/create messes.

What makes you regal is not how tall you stand or how you kiss a hand but being SEPARATE from em.

As social manipulators women are horrible in what they do to/say about us— please speak on this.

The copycat shooter will be another 24 year old who can't get a girlfriend and worships Satan.

He will watch shoot em up video games all day too, it's all entirely predictable.

Evil is here: civilization is unravelling, people are becoming corrupt, illegitimacy is massive.

YOUR WORK IS GOD'S FOR THIS TIME

You know your work comes from God so stay humble with glory to Him or you could lose it all.

LIBERAL WITCHES

God's got the End planned just as He did the beginning so relax into its Completion.

Handle completion like a crate of eggs: caution, move slowly, every move must be perfect.

Herein completes 100 books on how people screw you up: Its subtle but powerful, a terrible punch.

The resistances to liberty and true genius were crazy and I mal-adapted in a series of tragedies.

Now I'm free and protected in marriage but there was a dangerous time in which I was targeted.

Even the churches sought to make me conform to them or to go to their boring events.

Everyone sought to control me but it was before computers when they got into their own thing.

I'll ruminate no more on the tedious details of recent happenings for I know it's just prophesy.

I gotta mentally release this present era cuz it stinks and most people are out to get ya.

THE PATH TO GENIUS: FORGET IT

Let everything that happened when young implode like a marshmallow then disperse like a vapor.

The path to genius is learning how to manage people who want to manage you and your time.

For they all want a piece of you and get angry when you just want you: the path of the few.

Unfortunately it is not till we're elderly that we're finally free, a tragic joke if you ask me.

LIBERAL WITCHES

They call your words "crap" meaning they don't agree. It's hard on the sensitive so I'll ignore thee.

God made me a prolific writer but only by suffering disaster, exploding open emotions faster.

Brad Pitt, a world famous actor said he never read their reviews. For twenty years he refused.

DON'T LET THEM IN!

I sensed callous cruelty and disregard in the pests, a type of neglect like they couldn't care less.

But they're plenty into self, they can always make time for that. They can't be relied on, brats.

Self-realization is great, get into your talents and spend all your time on that if you want.

If it's wrong it's wrong, if it's right it's right--no lukewarm ever again, day and night.

We're "white supremacists" because we wanna live, endure and not be killed?

The Anti-God Party: What God condemns they affirm and what God punishes they exalt.

Crime, destruction, killing, robbin' and rapin: Most people wouldn't want them in.

Liberals fight by spreading it around. They're leaks to the streets cuz they're so low down.

Walking on eggshell environments: filled with anxiety we feel we're living in a grenade range.

First you internalize "I do not matter" then it's a feeling of shame and self-disgust as an adult later.

LIBERAL WITCHES

Ignored by family: I don't matter. Then shame and self-disgust automatically follows later.

Program: "I'm not good enough, there's something wrong with me" compels bad behavior, see?

The shame and disgust is so intense as an adult as it explodes recurrently and cripples us.

OSTRACIZNG

Then of course they hate him more and shun, bringing more shame as he's ostracized from the clan.

You learned shame in relationships in which you were devalued and this was internalized.

Not feeling good in our skin--as a human with needs--is a byproduct of this shame system.

It's less about immigration than it is our IDENTITY in the future, liable to disintegration.

In Europe you can't call them "rape squads" but rather "Asian local men"--help us God!

Either we connect through limbic resonance or the relationship has a profoundly sad emptiness.

If it's not part of the family culture, it's rules, core beliefs or skill set it's not gonna happen.

Sometimes we gotta make those decisions that break our heart but will heal our soul.

The integrity of the upright will guide them but the perversity of the unfaithful will destroy them.

YOU'RE NOT GOOD IF YOU SLEEP AROUND

LIBERAL WITCHES

You're not "good" if you sleep around and besides Jesus said NO one's good but God.

Riches don't profit in the day of wrath but righteousness delivers from death. Prov 11:4

The righteousness of the blameless will direct his way aright but the wicked will fall all by himself.

The righteousness of the upright will deliver them but the unfaithful will be caught by their own lust.

The righteous is delivered from trouble and it comes to the wicked instead. Prov 11:8.

INTERPERSONAL DISSONANCE IS PAIN

Nervous system is provoked cuz I feel the dissonance, the disconnect or the emotional distance.

I'm not going to endure attachment distress which reflects in the nervous system as pain/chaos.

Multinational Chicoms are behind the Trump-is-a-white-supremacist don't-come-to-El-Paso scam.

Tell a wise man or keep silent, because the mass man will mock it right away. Goethe

Globalism hates borders, by definition.

A took a lifetime of thrill-seeking to realize what I needed was PEACE not happiness.

It took many bad relationships to realize what I wanted and needed was STABILITY not looks/riches.

It took a lifetime of irksome social mal-adaptations to the rude to realize I needed solitude.

LIBERAL WITCHES

The lone thinker goes very deep but the conformist liberal stinker remains a shallow creep.

VALUE OF LEISURE VS. TOO MUCH WORK

Stop trying so hard for achievement. Relax into it, just do what's in front of you and enjoy it.

You're accomplishing TOO much. You're creating too fast--relax into it, let them slowly peruse it.

Would-be genius has an incapacity for leisure which is necessary to be a true genius.

An incapacity for leisure: work, work, work! I slowly realized I was trying to avoid mom's smirk.

True genius knows its UNDERGROUND work, fertile anarchy: creativity is doing nothing, leisurely.

Seek LEISURE then you're inspired. Just when I take the day off I'm ultra-creative, never tired.

Just continue doing exactly what you're doing and there's nothing done, nothing left undone.

We're either tunnel-visioned and work-focused or with wide diffuse perception: relaxed.

The gross male or jezebel will TAKE CONTROL the minute you give an em the chance: hell!

In an instant the Jezebel will take away all your self-will and powers. Please, watch out for her.

This is the true meaning of "rising up against you" in the bible. It's all about system reversals.

If you've had power and begin to slip, they'll reverse everything in a very painful, humiliating flip.

LIBERAL WITCHES

What I had to go thru because I was dense in certain areas--my Ph.D. in the streets in America.

MORALITY LEARNED THE HARD WAY

If parents don't teach it in the home, it takes 100 times more pain before you learn it on your own.

People are cruel and grabby from broken homes and then they create more without real love.

NOT BORN THAT WAY

Just cuz Conversion Therapy causes problems is no reason for Christians to accept the wrong.

FORGET how much they imposed on you and just be grateful for all that you learned from it.

Because weak men accept wrong as right, their countries are being taken from them, oh my.

A Christian can never agree that God made em that way since it's abomination and they're unfree.

SEE the direct connection between sin and the trouble in life and your hopes are revived.

Don't do what many Christians do: downplay sin until you're convinced wrong is right.

Mom instilled a hatred of men. After much trouble I returned to the father and life went better then.

MARRIAGE IS A FENCE, AT LAST

Dear parents: Please forgive me that I resented your conservative views, now I'm that way too.

Marriage--which feminist see as bondage--is the way for greatest female freedom for us.

LIBERAL WITCHES

Stop talking about conservative vs liberal and get down to the right point: what is MORAL?

You can't accept that Jesus died for forgiveness of sins, and then sin--that's a setup from Satan.

Single, it was drudgery to keep people away or make em behave but now it's easy, I'm amazed.

My husband is my fence and for the FIRST time in life I'm free, I can flourish and just be me.

Without a fence they come right up to your door and that's TOO CLOSE, I wanna keep em afar.

The minute I got married all harassment stopped and EVERYONE treated me differently--ole!

Marriage isn't 1 + 1 = 2 but rather = 20,000 when you consider all the opportunities/interconnections.

Tho' it was torture I HAD to be imposed on to learn all these precious and important lessons.

They say marriage reduplicates childhood for a woman and I agree, it's all about protection.

It's all in the approach: Be nice, sweet, end every sentence with "honey" and don't cheat.

Clean/order his office then leave him alone. Set him up in sweetness and he'll protect your home.

Being sweet makes him happy so he'll provide but starting fights blocks this as homelife dies.

KEEP SWEET AND HE'LL PROTECT YOUR RETREAT

Whatever you tell him will set his mind's direction so be careful and think before approachin'

LIBERAL WITCHES

I take him his bacon or melon with a sweet salutation then leave him to think, alone on his throne.

He's so happy he becomes productive. It reminds him of mom but it's better being above it.

Make him a happy, routined and structured home and he'll go to work to protect it from harm.

Stop being the center of attention for your "needs" met--that's the end of home life, get it?

STOP being a dam feminist demanding your rights--it's such a turn off, get out of yourself!

Men: STOP being a dam feminist, it's embarrassing. It's the ORDER of God you should be reflecting.

God's order is God over man, man over woman, woman over children: now DO it man.

Don't make your family so important that you cave in to evil--because then it's all over people.

Your spiritual family is most important--they are your sisters and brothers and they're abundant.

Don't worship "family" but then stay quiet {not stepping on toes} for then it's sin, ruin, riot.

SIN: TRASH BIN RUINED YOUR KIN

Tell em: "You're not born that way, you just love your sins but you can change and be happy"

If you love family take the chance to be rejected by it by standing against sin the ruiner of it.

Love, cherish and order your home. To appreciate it, think of the horribleness of homelessness.

LIBERAL WITCHES

You DON'T love family if you agree with sin/let em sink in their swill but repentance is a thrill.

For once morality is gone in a nation it will NEVER come back, as said Thomas Jefferson.

After I'm gone I pray someone will listen to this: Repent for BLISS for sin only ruins us.

GRANDMA: JUSTIFYING SIN IS NOT LOVIN'

Once you're is agreement that God made em that way, they're stuck and it's your fault, ok?

The moment you agree with evils you're overtaken and will find yourself accepting more of em.

Sin puts in in the dark and like a magnet attracts sharks who will kill you with hostile remarks.

Go ahead and sin all you want, whoremongers! Your future is laid out for you in hellish torture.

Sex sin is the greatest prognosticator of poverty and yet it's totally minimized in this century.

How dare you minimum these filthy sins between strangers--you have a very bleak future.

Sex is sacred and you blaspheme it with strangers so God will spit you out in disgust I wager.

A nation of justifiers of whores and whoremongers is going down fast in a house of horrors.

How could you be loving Grandma, justifying sins when you know better as an American?

From unwanted guests to foreign occupation, we must suffer to realize the value of freedom.

LIBERAL WITCHES

Some people are joy addicts with a continuous frozen smile on their face which seems fixed.

But hit a nerve and they come unglued--much worse cuz it's breaking their social device too.

BLESSED SEED AND GENIUS CHRISTIANS

Our greatest witness is a healed and complete life, our greatest distress is resentments, rife.

A seed of everything God is comes into us the MOMENT we receive Christ.

This special seed of God is the reason most scientific discoveries were made by Christians.

As we water that seed with the word of God and as our mind is renewed our work becomes "cool"

Another fruit of the spirit is forbearance: our ability to put up with stuff that is aggravating us.

Also discipline: To do what you know you should do when you don't feel like it at all.

Discipline is strength to do the things we should do in order to have the thing we want.

God leads us to do things never done before, opposite to others or what no one understands.

It's in my cowdog's DNA to watch the cat because animals don't see size differentials I guess.

I know the quip is right by how I feel in the body: a sense of completion and it's very groovy.

It's just me, the computer and the bank. No other interactions for in the past it stank.

LIBERAL WITCHES

I didn't feel right unless I felt I was wrong. My guilt was my self-punishment all along.

We don't need a plan but be led by the holy ghost and don't be addicted to reasoning, even worse.

Its the **END** that matters, not all you went thru to get here--that's all been forgiven for sure.

CHANGE OF SEASONS

Don't worry over memory for when that lesson is learned the whole era is dissolved.

Let the cycle complete itself naturally, never force it. Seasonal changes are unforced, face it.

Whenever you return to work think "you're producing too fast" and that'll make you relax.

Whenever you think of him/her you feel pain and emptiness so realize it's over **THEN** success.

Take the day off then torrents--floods--of creativity takes off, incessantly without pause.

Seasons change. You have seasons of putting yourself back together after being deranged.

You have seasons of learning the lessons about people and these are really horrible.

You have seasons of regrouping after a challenge and then flourishing/bringing yourself out.

You have seasons of enjoyment of fruits of thy labor after a lifetime of work/trying to gain favor.

You're producing too fast, you've got to relax. it's like a compulsion--instead, have a blast.

LIBERAL WITCHES

Creative and landmark insights are gained only in leisure so you must relax for sure.

GOD HAS TO RELEASE IT

God has to release it so stop looking to people for it cuz they're dumb as rocks or distracted.

As I complete my life's work I return to before it began. Fascinating viewing the whole span.

I'm enjoying old movies of the era of my birth. This is eldering: culling the past for pearls.

I gotta mentally get out of this present era cuz it stinks and most people think rinky-dink.

Perfect, beautiful and artistic old movies in beautiful sets: what a wonderful break from politics.

I'm going to pass sooner not later so I leave you these books, a Manual for Superior men not kooks.

OLD DIET THOUGHTS ON AUTOIMMUNITY

Crow in the morning, the crickets at night, a breeze in the afternoon all from my living room.

From my upstairs nest I look out at the red mountains and thank God for this view: astounding!

Afternoon snacks: Either almond butter and honey or a berry and coconut cream smoothie.

I avoid oxalates, lectins and goitrogens: no vegetables or greens just fruit or meat.

No oxalates (greens), lectins (beans) nor goitrogens (veggies)--the things we're told to eat.

LIBERAL WITCHES

What (strong) woman wears bacon grease and what man would allow it if he's a false religious?

It's a matter of total load--it's a budget. If I don't eat I'm never in reaction--that's the gist.

NEW DIET THOUGHTS: JUICE/BEANS/RICE

Beans and rice that's it. I filled the basement with such as this and that's the proper family storage miss.

Anything else can be scavenged from the environment: fruits, greens, supergreens, seeds/nuts.

Now I've adapted to beans/rice I feel really good. NO FAT for two weeks and I feel and look like I should.

Bananas/raisins in rice milk with cane sugar and collagen. That's my sugar breakfast and I'm flying high again.

For brunch have refried beans with minced onions/salsa. Or pumpernickel bread with fruit spreads--lotsa.

Midnight to 6 am it's juices then I hit the solid fruits then beans. It scrapes the intestine/I'm a beanpole it seems.

Fruit and grains: the most basic diet, it's biblical and all cultures enjoy same for superior health mainly.

Not fruit and greens. Greens won't sustain you, they're only what you scavenge in addition to the storage below.

FATS CREATE WRINKLES? DEBATE

All the fats I loaded up on for years--avocados, cheese, "healthy" oils, butters--the basis of wrinkles/tears.

All those "good" fats cling to the inner skin--they line it and it crinkles, called wrinkles and ugly adipose.

LIBERAL WITCHES

At first it seems the cheese/fats oil the skin but it CREATES the false body of ugly skin protuberances: yikes.

When fully detoxed from old fats you won't need to moisturize the skin or eat fats to keep it healthy--it just IS.

I thought I needed the fats for satiety but with a detoxed belly from the grain scrapers I'm never hungry, truly.

I thought I needed all those nut butters and coco-creams. Good to have em in storage but way too oily for me.

Grains go sugary. High sugar, low fat: thin and healthy. Low sugar, high fat: skinny fat, not that jaunty.

FRUIT MAKES US CUTE

Since MacDougal recommended STARCH without fruit he looked washed out-- we NEED it to look cute.

They cured diabetes Type 2 100% with sugar, white rice, fruit and fruit juice.

Juice: apple. Fruit: banana/raisin. Misc: Rice milk, white sugar. Meals: corn/rice/cereal/pumpernickel.

Pumpernickel with fruit spreads, what could be more humble and it's acid-binding so it's also an achievement.

As long as I'm lowfat my perception stays bright in a cornucopic phantasmagoria and I'm fascinated.

With every lowfat meal you'll see the fading of wrinkles increasingly as previous fats are digested out.

Do I believe all this? Not really. Eat your fats but eat one meal a day and that fast will keep wrinkles away.

100 KAREN KELLOCK BOOKS

AFFINITY OR MISERY
AGELESS CORNUCOPIA
AMERICA AWAKE!
AMERICA'S DAFT ERA
ARTS OF PALEO FASTING
AUTOPHAGY ON CHEATERS
BACKSTABBING NEUROTICS
BETRAYAL TRAUMA
BOOMERS AND BROKENNESS
BOOT ON NECK
CHAMPION GUIDES
COMMIE NUTHOUSE
COMMIES
COMMUNIST SPIRIT
CONTAGION OF MADNESS
CONTAGIOUS MADNESS
CULTURE CLASH BASHED
DAFT LEFT
DAILY FASTARIAN
DAM RATS
DIVERSITY IS CRUELTY
E-RACE WHITE
EVIL FREAKS (Beyond Gross)
THE END OR A BEND?
FEMALE BULLIES AND FEMI-NAZIS
FEMALE CARNALITY
FEMALE DUMB DOWN
FEMALE POWER DRIVE
FEMINISM AND RUIN 1 & 2
FIX FOR MISFITS
FOOLS & TRAMPS
FREEDOM SPEAKING
FRENEMY ENABLER
FRENEMY LIAR
FRENEMY THIEF
FRENEMY TRAITOR
TRENEMY TYRANT
GENIUS IS HELD DOWN
GLOBALISLAM
GOD USES THE FLAWED
HAZE OF THE LATTER DAYS

KAREN KELLOCK PH.D.

M.S. Political Science, San Diego State. Ph.D. in Psychology, University of California Irvine. Postdoctoral: UCI School of Medicine, Dept. of Psychiatry [NIMH Grants].
Developed the Debris Theory of Disease, a theory of system pathology in 120 books and 22 textbooks for the general public. The theory has a general formula: All disease is obstruction, all recovery is elimination, all success is attraction. The three obstructions are people, habit and food. Remove obstruction and snap to your goals, waiting in the wings.